I0568443

I Hear His Voice Calling

A 14-Day Devotional to Hearing God

By:

Dr. Nikki Rader

Table of Contents

Dedication

This book is dedicated to my Father God, who placed this calling to write on my life many years ago, and lovingly guided me through the experiences He blessed me with in order to write this book.

And to my husband, who has supported me through the years it has taken to get to this point. Your unwavering confidence in my calling has been of the utmost importance.

INTRODUCTION

I remember it like it was yesterday, the white foam project board and flower stickers representing the words of God's voice calling me to write a book. It was before we, as personal computer owners, had easy access to graphic design tools. The words "I Hear His Voice Calling" have been etched in my mind and on my heart since that day, many years ago. Let me tell you; this path has been full of hope, excitement, discouragement, frustration, anger, revisions, twists, education, preparation, waiting, patience, and revelation. It is not what I thought it would be 20 years ago when I first got the call from God.

All my adult life, I have desired to be an author. I cannot remember a time in my life when writing a book has not been on my bucket list. I have lists of book ideas that God has laid on my heart. But for some reason, it is as though this part of my life has been stuck in quicksand. Sometimes the call from God has been so strong that the spirit overcomes me, and all I can do is bow down and be filled with ideas. But the frustrating part is that when that time is over, I do not have the strength to get up and write, and when I do, all of those ideas and words are gone.

Times like those mentioned above made me question whether I could take spiritual revelations and put them into words. How could God use someone like me who couldn't even remember what He had just said? My mind was jumbled. Nothing would come together when I would try to sit down and write. Frustration would take over. Do I quit? Did God get it wrong? Why would He put such a burning desire in my heart to rip it away?

But that isn't who Christ is, so what was the hold-up? What was standing between the call of Christ and me? I had the call, and I heard the call. Why wasn't it happening? Is God giving me more time to grow? Do I have areas in my life that need attention before moving on? Is Satan building these roadblocks to deter me from following God's calling? Is life getting in the way of my calling? But haven't I also been called to be a wife, mama, and Nahna? These are all things that have crossed my mind. Ten years later, I still had the same questions. Twenty years later, the questions still linger. How can it be 20 years later, and I find myself asking the same questions, finding myself no closer than I was when I first received the call?

When I received the initial call, I cannot remember what book I was reading. It was probably a Stormie Omartian, Becky Tirabassi, or Elizabeth George book; however, the call came upon me immediately. It was such a strong and overwhelming feeling. I remember going to the store and buying everything I needed for the project board. I got cute little stickers to help create the outline. One by one, I placed a flower followed by words made of stickers to represent each idea God had given me for chapters. I remember displaying it in my office and praying over the idea for weeks. I knew God had a purpose for me and that he would use me. Time passed, and I packed the project board away as I made room for new decorations and ideas. Still, every so often, the board would come to mind. I would take it out and look at it, praying God would give me the ability to begin writing.

Fast forward 20 years. God had a plan! Imagine that! God has taken me through a Bachelor's and Master's Degree in English and now a Doctorate in Organizational Leadership with an emphasis in Christian Ministries. He has led me to and through many situations that have grown me and taught me how to hear and know God's voice and His call(s) on my life. He has orchestrated events in my life and the life of my immediate family that I could have never made happen. He amazes me, and I cannot wait to share what God has done for me and taught me.

So, how do we hear God, and how do we know what we hear is from God? How do we follow through with what we hear Him say? How do we have and develop a relationship with God? To be able to hear God's calling on our life, we must listen to Him in our daily life. We will dig into the questions above, get some answers, and start hearing God's voice in our daily lives and our life's calling.

2 Peter 1:10, "Therefore, brethren, be all the more diligent

to make certain about His calling and choosing you; for as long as you practice these things, you will never stumble."

This 14-day plan will walk you step-by-step into a better understanding of how to hear and discern God's voice.

When answering the questions, meditate on each day. Try to purposefully see things you have talked with God about, and answer the questions based on that. Look back and see the blessings. Note that some questions are asked more than once. This is to remind you of the importance of specific actions.

DAY 1

I was saved at the age of 8. I went to church twice on Sunday and Wednesday nights. But inside, I was confused because I knew I was saved, but I did not understand what I was still missing. It was not until my mid to late 20's that I realized I was missing a relationship with God. I had gained access to this relationship when becoming saved but never tapped into it.

So, how do we have a relationship with God? I am talking about a daily communication kind of relationship with God. Think about our friendships/relationships. We like to have those people around us. We like to share our thoughts, plans, goals, and needs in life. We want to go to these people for advice and direction. All of that is good; God designed us to desire friendship. However, we must never forget that He created this need for friendship secondary to His relationship with us. Anything we might go to our friends or those we are in a relationship with, and even things we would keep to ourselves, God desires us to come to Him first.

Let's talk about how we start these conversations? Think again about our friendships/relationships. We didn't immediately tell our new friends everything. We didn't immediately recognize their voice in a crowd. It took time, time to get to know them. Getting to know people happens by starting with small conversations, their likes, families, etc. As we begin to visit with our new friends more, we learn what they like, how they might respond, and what their voice sounds like. We recognize them and their voice.

The same thing happens with God. Start talking to Him about small things: what road to take on your way home, what to eat, what to wear, the weather, a parking space, the world around you, what is going on with your friends and family, and other things that pop into your mind. You will begin to hear His voice the more you talk to Him.

"I love those who love me, and those who seek me diligently find me" Proverbs 8:17.

There are five people in the Bible that answered the call by saying to God, "Here I am." Each of these people were blessed exceedingly for being available to God. Choose one of the six or all six and read through their experiences. Spend a few days here if you need to or come back and read each of them when you have time:

Abraham- Genesis Chapter 22
Jacob- Genesis Chapter 31
Moses- Exodus Chapter 3
Samuel- 1 Samuel Chapter 3
Isaiah- Isaiah Chapter 6

Take a moment to reflect on your friendships/relationships. Write down, in the blank space below, how you met some of these individuals. What were the first things you talked about? How long did it take for you to trust them and have deeper conversations with them? How long did it take for you to know their voice without seeing their face? Now, write down a few small things you think you could talk to God about, no matter how silly it seems. Then if you are feeling bold in growing your relationship with the Lord, write down something big you need to hear from God.

DAY 2

It is essential to take time and evaluate barriers that might distract or even block us from hearing God's voice. Let's spend today looking at our own heart. Doing this will prepare us for the next 12 days. It will help open up the lines of communication with our Heavenly Father.

One thing I struggle with is my emotions. Often, I allow my emotions to overtake my faith. What we are doing over these next 13 days will be building our faith. You can bet there will be some doubts appear during these two weeks. It is inevitable. I have heard it said that "we often believe our doubt and doubt our beliefs." I have been guilty of that. This mindset must change. We need to tell our emotions to sit back and rest while our faith takes over.

I have experienced, in extreme trials, that having faith and living in faith is much more emotionally draining than letting the fear take over. This emotional draining happens because I am constantly regrouping and talking myself back into the realm of faith over worry. Fear is more effortless than faith. However, I noticed that when I do live in faith, even though emotionally taxing, I walk out of the trial much stronger than if I spent the entire time worrying.

Several Godly people in the Bible struggled with emotions

including David, Elijah, Jonah, Job, Moses, and others. Read Psalm 4 and Jonah Chapters 1-2.

Let's start today's evaluation of our hearts with this prayer from Psalm. "Test me, O Lord, and try me, examine my heart and my mind. For your love is ever before me, and I walk continually in your truth" Psalm 26: 2-3.

The following questions provide time for you to reflect on what God is saying to you. As you read through and answer the questions, open your mind and heart to the voice of God. I would even recommend praying and asking God to speak to you to help answer these questions.

1. In times of past trials, how have your emotions or other barriers played a role your faith?

_____

_____

_____

_____

_____

2. Have your emotions or other barriers oppressed your faith in times of trials or have you been able to have unwavering faith, explain your answer?

_____

_____

_____

_____

_____

3. What can you ask God to help you overcome these next two weeks in regards to your emotions or other barriers and your faith?

_____

_____

_____

_____

_____

4. Read the prayer again and write down the first positive idea or image that comes to your mind?

_____

_____

_____

_____

5. Now ask God to show you something He wants you to work on as we go through these next two weeks; say the prayer again, and write down the first thing that comes to your mind?

_____

_____

_____

_____

Continue to focus on the positive ideas God shared with you as well as the things God wants you to work on.

DAY 3

One of the key actions we will learn in hearing God's voice is to pray scripture over ourselves. After several years of praying scripture for each family member, this idea came to me. At one point, I heard God ask me, "How can you understand the importance of praying scripture over your family but not take time to pray scripture over yourself?" It was something that had never crossed my mind. I decided to pray that God would show me my scripture prayer. And, let me tell you, He did not disappoint. The prayer God gave me has sustained my husband and me through raising two children into adults, moving, starting new companies, purchasing investment properties, completing a doctorate's degree, and much more. Here is the prayer God gave me from Psalm 62:5-8 & 33:20-22. You can see how I have taken it and tailored it to say "my" and "I":

My soul finds rest in you alone, God, for You are where my hope comes from. You alone are my rock and my salvation you are my fortress; I will not be shaken. My salvation and my honor depend on you, Lord; you are my mighty rock, my refuge. I trust in you at all times; I pour my heart out to you, for you are my refuge. I wait and hope for you, Lord; you are my help and my shield. In you, my heart rejoices, for I trust your holy name. May your unfailing love rest upon me, Lord, even as I put my hope in you.

Find a scripture to pray over yourself today. Start in Psalm

15

if you do not have a life scripture already. Maybe you pray the scripture above over yourself today. Use the space below to write down a few scriptures. If God lays a scripture on your heart, write it out as your prayer. Personalize it to your life. This is a process that may take some time, but I encourage everyone to have a life scripture. Repeat this process every day until you find the scripture God has given you. Then continue to pray that every day.

_____

_____

_____

_____

_____

_____

_____

_____

_____

_____

_____

_____

_____

_____

DAY 4

I like to dress nice, and I want my clothes to fit well. When they don't, I get grouchy, and everyone around me suffers. That is no way for me to live or the people around me. So when I am feeling sensitive to this, I talk to God about it. I say, "God, you can see my emotions today, pick me out something to wear," and every time, it is perfect. Your grouchy may be something completely different. Regularly, I ask God the road to take home. I have learned to discern his voice over the years, and I take the road he sends me on. Sometimes it may be the long way, but I assure you it is the best way.

I am not sure what God's voice sounds like to you, but for me, after years of talking to God, it is a still small voice within. I ask God a question, and I have to be entirely open to the answer. The first thing that pops into my mind is God's answer. This takes time and commitment to learning His voice. His answer might be yes, no, or silence. He might say take the long way home. He might say, you will pay $X for an investment property.

You may be wondering about my desires getting in the way. Our desires can prove an issue if we do not keep them in check with God. If my worldly ways try to sway me to think God is telling me something I want to hear, I have immediate conviction. My chest physically hurts. Then I know I am trying to make God do what I want instead of His will. It is a humbling and sorrowful feeling, but it is a beautiful moment when repentance immediately follows. It is essential that when listening to God for direction, we make sure our hearts are right and aligned with God. Of course, this should be how we want to live always, but let's be honest. We sin, all of us. So, we must continually work to align and live a life seeking righteousness.

The more difficult things I talk with God about consist of friendship/relationship problems, people I struggle with but want to love, scripture meaning, and what to say to people before I have a conversation with them. I also talk to God about what to write in my devotions and books, finances, investments, my husband and I being united in God's direction, my children and grandchildren, my calling, and many other things as they arise.

"The Lord, your God, is in your midst, a mighty one who will save; he will rejoice over you with gladness; he will quiet you by His love; he will exult over you with loud singing" Zephaniah 3:17.

It can seem awkward at first; God is okay with that, and I promise you, the more you talk with Him, the more you hear Him. It will bring great joy to your life as you realize your creator loves you so much that he wants to talk to you and answer your questions. It will put a smile on your face.

Read Genesis Chapter 3 and take note to the simplicity and conversational tone of our Lord, Adam, and Eve. It was a difficult time, but God carried on a conversation with them just as we would have.

Today, let's take some time talking to God. Try to have a conversation with God like you would with a friend. Remember, He created us for companionship. He walked with Adam and Eve, visiting with them about their day. He wants to do the same with you. Write down how you felt about this visit with God.

_____

_____

_____

_____

_____

_____

_____

Now, write down how you would like to feel when you visit with God. Ask God to help you be more comfortable talking to Him. Remember, it is okay to go to God in reverence, awe, and praise. Still, it is okay to go to God for simple yet meaningful conversation.

_____

_____

DAY 5

I have experienced God keeping His promises to me throughout my life, so why is it so difficult to follow the call of God and step out of my comfort box at times? As I consider this question, two things come to mind. The first reason is that I keep so busy that life drowns out the call of God. I allow my days to be filled with so many tasks to accomplish that I leave no room to hear God calling me. Even when I do hear it, many times, it is just a quick whisper that I allow to pass through my mind and heart just as any regular thought might.

The second reason following the call of God is difficult stems from the reliance on my comfort zone. Satan has the expert ability to convince me things will go wrong if I step out of my comfort zone and follow the call of Christ. If I am willing to act immediately, I will not allow Satan time to distract me. Why in the world would I allow Satan to control my comfort zone instead of letting the God of the universe, who holds me, provides for me, designs a path specifically for me, and keeps His promises to control where I am comfortable.

Because of Abraham's faith to go and believe, a nation was blessed **(Hebrews 11:8-13)**. One act of obedience to the call of Christ blessed an entire nation. David followed the call of God and conquered Goliath **(1 Samuel 17)**. God blessed David and considered him "a man after His own heart" **(1 Samuel 13:14)**.

Ruth followed the call to stay with Naomi **(Ruth 1)**. God blessed her and placed her in the direct lineage of Christ. Saul gave his life to Christ and became Paul, who followed the call of God that helped shape and share what we read and believe today. Throughout the Bible, we see many individuals stepping up by Faith and following God because they believe in His promises. God's promises are not just for those in the Bible; they are for each of us. If, when God calls, we step out on faith and believe, He will keep His promises to us and move in ways we never thought possible. I encourage you today to step out of your comfort zone with Faith that God is who He says He is and does what He says He will do.

In 1 Kings 18, we read about Elijah, Obadiah, Ahab, and Baal's prophets. Elijah's experience is of great importance in following the call of God and the outcome of obedience. Elijah heard God call him and tell him to go to Ahab because of the great drought. There are four steps to following God's call that Obadiah used. We will cover one a day for the next four days. Let's take a look. Read 1 Kings 18: 1-8.

Step 1: Immediate obedience

Elijah didn't wait around. He didn't discuss it with God. God said go, and Elijah went. This step gets a little easier each time you step out in obedience. Elijah knew that delayed obedience was disobedience.

On his way, Elijah ran into Obadiah. Obadiah was in charge of Ahab's palace, and he was a believer in the Lord. He had hidden one hundred prophets in two caves as protection from Jezebel's order to kill all of the prophets of the Lord. Obadiah had been looking for Elijah because Ahab felt Elijah was the cause of the drought. When Elijah saw Obadiah, he told him to tell Ahab that he was here to see him.

The following questions provide time for you to reflect on what God is saying to you. As you read through and answer the questions, open your mind and heart to the voice of God. I would even recommend praying and asking God to speak to you to help answer these questions.

1. What can you commit to doing to build your relationship with God today?

_____

_____

_____

_____

_____

_____

2. What small thing could you ask God to answer for you?

_____

_____

_____

_____

_____

3. What can you ask God to help you with today?

_____

_____

_____

_____

4. What actions can you take to be immediately obedient, or is there anything you need to be obedient to God about today?

_____

_____

_____

_____

5. How have you experience God in your life?

_____

_____

_____

_____

_____

6. What can you thank God for today?

_____

_____

_____

_____

_____

DAY 6

I find great importance in hearing God's voice and following God's call on my life. I also find magnificent joy and excitement in seeing God's direction come to fruition in my life and the lives of those around me. God often prepares us in advance for something He is asking us to do. We may find ourselves in a season of waiting. I have found that doubt and worry can creep in during the waiting. I find it incredibly frustrating and irritating that I allow this to happen, especially since I have experienced God's provisions all of my life. I have story after story and month after month of experiencing God's provisions. Yet, there are times that worry creeps in. Questions such as, "Is God going to continue to provide, Doesn't He get tired of providing, how in the world could He provide this?"

It is also important to remember that other people may doubt or question what you say is a calling from God. Don't be alarmed or deterred by this. You must remember that they were not there with you when you heard from God. God doesn't always share your calling with others. So you may be the only one that got the message. However, there may be times when God shares your calling with someone else, and that person is sent to confirm God's calling's on your life. Either way, you must heed what God says, not what others think.

What is important to remember is that we are not alone in the waiting, and we are not alone in the things God asks us to do. God is there; He is working behind the scene on our behalf. Throughout scripture, we can see this with Abraham, Noah, Jonah, Joshua, Samuel, Esther, Job, David, Solomon, Daniel, Joseph, Mary, all the Disciples, and Paul. We can trust God to help us. I saw a picture with the saying below, which convicted my heart.

Trust = Consistency/Time.

Isn't that so true? God is consistent time and time again to provide, so we can always trust God without fear. When we allow fear to creep in, we begin to cause havoc on ourselves and those around us. Read 1 Kings 18: 9-15.

Step 2: Push through the opposition

Focus on God's voice and what God calls you to do, not what others say to distract you. Don't let someone else's fears become yours.

When Elijah saw Obadiah, he told Obadiah to tell Ahab that he, Elijah, was here to see him. Immediately Obadiah was consumed with fear and doubt. He begged for mercy through self-proclamation. Obadiah said, "Ahab will kill me because we have looked for you, and you have been nowhere. Now when I go tell him, who knows if you will still be here. Don't you know what I have done for God? I have saved 100 prophets."

Obadiah was fearful for his life, and he tried to dissuade Elijah from his course. We all know people like this. We may even be this person at times. Obadiah was afraid that the Spirit of the Lord would lead Elijah from that place and that Ahab would kill him when they could not find Elijah. But Elijah promised that he would be there.

Push through the opposition. Stay the course!
Great blessings are awaiting you!

The following questions provide time for you to reflect on what God is saying to you. As you read through and answer the questions, open your mind and heart to the voice of God. I would even recommend praying and asking God to speak to you to answer these questions.

1. How did you hear God yesterday, and how did He answer your questions about the small things?

_____

_____

_____

_____

_____

2. What can you commit to do to build your relationship with God today?

_____

_____

_____

_____

_____

3. Is there anyone or anything that is causing opposition to you hearing God's voice or His call?

_____

_____

_____

_____

_____

4. What can you ask God to help you with today?

_____

_____

_____

_____

_____

5. What did you learn from God the last few days?

_____

_____

_____

_____

_____

6. How have you experience God in your life?

_____

_____

_____

_____

_____

7. What can you thank God for today?

_____

_____

_____

_____

_____

8. Just a reminder to pray scripture over yourself. Feel free to write it here.

_____

_____

_____

_____

_____

DAY 7

There are a lot of wonderfully enlightening experiences to read in the Bible. But for quite some time now, the experience of the sick woman who touches Jesus' robe in Mark 5 draws me in. She exemplifies four characteristics that we should all want to possess.

- Doubtless Faith- She touched Jesus' robe believing, without doubt, that touching His robe would heal her.
- Immediate acceptance of Jesus' gift of healing- She didn't wait to get home to realize she had been healed. She recognized immediately.
- Owning up to choices even when you don't know how people will respond- She didn't know if Jesus would be upset for touching Him, but she came and fell at His feet and explained everything to Him.
- Healed by Faith- Jesus said to her, "Daughter, your faith has healed you, go in peace and be freed from your sufferings."

Oh, to say the name of Jesus, believe it, and receive the gift He gives. Read 1 Kings 18:16-41.

Step 3: Extreme Faith

Elijah was a man of extreme faith. His faith begins to show in these verses when he calls out the prophets of God for their wavering and fear. If that wasn't enough, he challenged the 450 prophets of Baal.

When their God doesn't answer, what does Elijah do? He begins to taunt the prophets of Baal, yet Baal does not respond. Then, extreme faith takes over. Elijah not only prepares his bull, but he also drenches the offering and wood with water three different times! Finally, Elijah prays, and the Lord answers.

Something I have learned over the years is that God finds delight in answering our prayers. He isn't scared or offended by our prayers, no matter how big they are. Actually, God looks forward to what we consider our bigger and bolder prayers. Why? Because in our asking, we are giving God opportunities to show off His mightiness. I encourage you to dream big. God didn't create you to be scared of Him; He created you to reach out and let Him use you to further His Kingdom. So, let's be Kingdom builders.

The following questions provide time for you to reflect on what God is saying to you. As you read through and answer the questions, open your mind and heart to the voice of God. I would even recommend praying and asking God to speak to you to help answer these questions.

1. How did you hear God yesterday, and how did He answer your questions about the small things?

_____

_____

_____

_____

_____

2. What can you commit to do to build your relationship with God today?

_____

_____

_____

_____

_____

3. What can. You do today or soon that requires extreme faith?

_____

_____

_____

_____

_____

4. What is God calling you to do to be a Kingdom builder?

_____

_____

_____

_____

_____

5. How have you experience God in your life?

_____

_____

_____

_____

6. What can you thank God for today?

_____

_____

_____

_____

7. Pray the same scripture over yourself from yesterday or find a new scripture if you like.

_____

_____

_____

_____

_____

DAY 8

We are over halfway there, and I am sure you have experienced it, DOUBT! So, let's take a day to process through our doubt. Then, we will move back into Step 5.

Sometimes it is easy to doubt God's voice. Because many times we feel utterly unprepared for the path God is taking us down or the calls God puts on our lives. Even Moses, one of the greatest Bible heroes, expressed his fear of inability to live out the calling God had on his life.

Sometimes we may not feel equipped to follow God's voice. We may not feel educated enough or even know where to begin. Our inabilities may be evident to all of those around us, but God sees things through different eyes. He sees what He created us to be, not what we allow the world to tell us we are.

Moses decided to take the leap of faith and trust in God's call for his life. And, God provided everything he needed. God does not expect us to have everything perfectly prepared to hear and follow His voice. If that were the case, we would not need His help. What God desires is a heart of obedience, a heart willing to free fall into the unknown, so we can experience the miracles of God's amazing plans for us.

Do not be afraid to take that leap of faith, and do not be dismayed if the voice of God in your life looks different from what you expected. Often, we limit ourselves only seeing what is right in front of us, but God sees our entire future. He knows exactly where we are going and how to get us there. He knows what is best, and He is ready to do amazing work through us.

"Therefore, my brothers, be all the more eager to make your calling and election sure. For if you do these things, you will never fall..." 2 Peter 1:10.

Are you feeling alone, left, or forgotten? Don't! God is chasing after you to give you strength. Remember, when we side with God, we are the majority because God is more significant than any number of people.

Read John 20:24-29 and Judges Chapter 6, and you will find Godly people in the Bible also struggled with doubt. If you keep reading, you will also find that God always comes through.

The following questions provide time for you to reflect on what God is saying to you. As you read through and answer the questions, open your mind and heart to the voice of God. I would even recommend praying and asking God to speak to you to help answer these questions.

1. Take a minute and ask God what your purpose is. You can choose short-term, long-term, professional life, personal life, or anything you would like. Remember that throughout your life, parts of

your purpose can change. Write down what He says to you. It may be small bits and pieces that may not make complete sense yet, or it may be exact with great understanding.

_____

_____

_____

_____

_____

2. What are some decisions you are afraid to make?

_____

_____

_____

_____

_____

3. What makes you feel like quitting?

_____

_____

_____

_____

_____

4. What can you ask God to help you with today to overcome your doubt?

_____

_____

_____

_____

5. Pray scripture over yourself today.

_____

_____

_____

_____

_____

DAY 9

"For I know the plans I have for you, says the Lord." This verse is one of the most comforting scriptures in the Bible, yet I struggle with it often. Several years ago, my husband and I decided I should leave my job. Although we felt God led us to that decision, it was challenging to do. We have had many ups and downs since that time. But, we press on.

We fix our eyes on the Lord because we know he works in our lives. We have experienced his hand in our lives many times. We must embrace this moment and try to understand better who God is and what he wants to teach us because there are no purposeless moments in life.

If you struggle with a sense of purposelessness, seek God for the direction. I love the New Living Translation of Matthew 7:7, "Keep on asking, and you will receive what you ask for. Keep on seeking, and you will find. Keep on knocking, and the door will be opened to you." Read 1 Kings 42-46.

Step 4: Perseverance/Persistence

This might be my favorite part of Elijah's story here because it is the characteristic I admire most about him. "..., but Elijah climbed to the top of Carmel, bent down to the ground, and put his face between his knees." He knew what he was asking the Lord to do was huge. He knew it was only going to happen by an act of the Lord. Not one, or two, or three, but seven times he sent his servant to look for a sign of rain. Finally, on the seventh time, a cloud appeared. He had unwavering, persistent faith that God would do what He said He would do.

How often do we have this faith? Do you find yourself giving up after your third or fourth time asking? I encourage you to be persistent. Commit to the Lord that you are here for the long haul. Are you desperate enough to get up early, carve some time at lunch, open your Bible, and pray at bedtime instead of turning on the TV? Show God you believe He is who He says He is.

The following questions provide time for you to reflect on what God is saying to you. As you read through and answer the questions, open your mind and heart to the voice of God. I would even recommend praying and asking God to speak to you to help answer these questions.

1. How have you been hearing God, and what has He been saying to you?

_____

_____

_____

_____

2. What can you commit to doing to build your relationship with God today?

_____

_____

_____

_____

3. What is happening or coming up that will require extreme faith?

_____

_____

_____

_____

4. What might this extreme faith look like?

_____

_____

_____

_____

5. What did you learn from God today?

_____

_____

_____

_____

6. Is there something you need to commit to God for an answer?

_____

_____

_____

_____

7. What can you thank God for today?

_____

_____

_____

_____

8. Pray the same scripture over yourself from yesterday or find a new scripture if you like.

_____

_____

_____

_____

_____

DAY 10

There comes a time when we want to hear real-life examples of how God speaks to others in hopes of identifying God's voice in our own life. My dearest friend, who is growing in her relationship with the Lord and learning His voice for the first time, had a supernatural encounter with Him.

In her prayer and journaling time, she began to express to God that she needed to hear His voice. Although she had been a Christian for quite some time and tried to follow what she knew to be right, she had never heard God's voice, and she felt quite a bit of sorrow about situations in her life. She thought to herself, "How can I hear Your voice, God, if I do not even know what it sounds like?" So again, she gave God her request to speak to her in a way that she would know it was God.

The next day she got up and went about her usual routine. She was sitting in the car waiting, and she decided to listen to a podcast. This podcast was talking about Leah and Rachel. The podcast discussed Leah and her ability to gain peace with God, and was now focused on how Rachel dealt with a sorrowful heart. My friend was identifying with Rachel; she felt like Rachel that day. At the exact time the podcast was discussing Rachel's story, my friend received a text from an unknown phone number, and the text said. "Hi, Rachel; trying to see if you get this message. I love the sunshine today!" My friend's name is NOT Rachel!

Wow! Supernatural Intervention!

She knew the sound of God's voice immediately through that message, and she knew that God was telling her to focus on the good and let the sorrow go! All she could do was smile and say, "I hear you, God!" How amazing is God? He used what may have been a wrong number to reach my friend! He cares so much. He will do whatever it takes to reach us.

There are several ways God speaks to us. Here are a few:

SCRIPTURE:

God's Word can give us direction in every situation we encounter. Romans 10:17 says, "Consequently, faith comes from hearing the message, and the message is heard through the word about Christ." God's Word is alive. He can use the same verse to guide us in many different situations. I have experienced God using scripture to help my husband and I buy property. I pray scripture over each of my family members. I recently asked God to give me a scripture for my granddaughter, who struggles with unpleasant dreams. Within minutes, He led me to Proverbs 3:24, "When you lie down, you will not be afraid; when you lie down, your sleep will be sweet."

STILL SMALL VOICE:

This one is a little more difficult to describe to people who have never experienced it. The still small voice comes in the form of a feeling or thought. At first, this was concerning to me. What if I misinterpret God's voice? I have learned over the years that if I misinterpret God's voice either by accident or personal persuasion, I feel the tug of conviction. Conviction is how I know if what I hear is God's voice and my decision is from God or my desires. As I grew closer to God, I begin to feel Him. When I ask for an answer or to know that it is Him speaking or orchestrating a moment, I get what I would call chills. They are similar to chills you get when you are cold but much more supernatural. I would say even trance generating. 1 Kings 19:12 is an excellent supporting scripture of hearing a still small voice, "And after the earthquake a fire; but the Lord was not in the fire: and after the fire a still small voice. And it was so, when Elijah heard it, that he wrapped his face in his mantle, and went out, and stood in the entering in of the cave."

WORSHIP:

There is just something about the supernatural power of God through worship. I am not a crier, but I no longer wear mascara to church because, during worship, I am most generally moved to tears. I receive that same supernatural chill during worship. There are song lyrics that say, "I can see the evidence of your goodness all over my life, all over my life." When I hear this song, God takes me back to visions of this evidence throughout my life.

48

Colossians 3:16-17 says, "Let the word of Christ richly dwell within you, with all wisdom teaching and admonishing one another with psalms and hymns and spiritual songs, singing with thankfulness in your hearts to God. Whatever you do in word or deed, do all in the name of the Lord Jesus, giving thanks through Him to God the Father."

VISIONS:

Visions come in several forms; this is just a shortlist. Visions can often be spiritual perceptions that lead to a quick image of something that might happen, identifying something wrong, needs to be changed, or even something great. Sometimes we may experience an image that moves quickly in and out of our minds or even dreams. Acts 18:9, "One night the Lord spoke to Paul in a vision: "Do not be afraid; keep on speaking, do not be silent." Another vision that I have experienced is appearance. I will be reading a book, article, or webpage, look down to make a note of what I just read, then look back up, and it is gone. I recognize this as a message from God. These are ideas God wants to convey to me, but they do not last long, just long enough for me to see. These appearances remind me of King Belshazzar's experience with the writing on the wall and interpretation by Daniel in Daniel chapter 5 (except my experiences have been positive). However, now we have the Holy Spirit to translate or open our eyes to see the message God is sending us.

ANGELS:

Sometimes, when God speaks, He does so through Angels. Several years ago, my friend lost her sister. While at the hospital, my friend went to the rooftop to get away from everyone. On the rooftop, she met a woman who informed her that her sister was now healed. When she went back down to the ER, her sister had passed. Later, when talking with her mom, my friend realized the lady she had seen had the same name as her sister's childhood imaginary friend. It was then that my friend realized she had seen an angel, and her sister was in Heaven. Angels are mentioned throughout the Bible, and Acts 8:26 is a great example. "Now, an angel of the Lord said to Philip, "Go south to the road — the desert road — that goes down from Jerusalem to Gaza."

ORCHESTRATION:

We must have our eyes open and our hearts ready to hear God's voice within the circumstances. The fall of Jericho in Joshua chapter 6 is a great reference of orchestration. My experience came when we moved to our new town; a brick building caught my eye. I envisioned owning this building. Over three years, the building would be emptied then filled back up with a new business, but nothing ever seemed to last. As a church, we started reading and studying Circle Maker by Mark Batterson. I started praying about the Brick Building. I followed the 21-day prayer and added fasting to the 21 days. I desired to know beyond a shadow of a doubt that this was God's plan. As I prayed, God began to speak to me. He told me that, yes, this was to be our Brick Building, and He gave me a specific purchase price. On my way home from church, I noticed a lady standing in front of the Brick Building, working on a sign. I drove past the building but felt the urge of the Holy Spirit to turn back around. So, I did. I asked if she knew if the building was for sale. She told me it was for sale, and she showed me around. I finally got up the nerve to ask her the price of the building. She softly said I am asking…, and her words produced the exact amount God had told me we would pay. I immediately teared up. This was God; there was no doubt about it. I told her that I had been praying. She interrupted me and said, "You are a Christian?" Her question caught me off guard, but I said, "Yes, I am a Christian." And then she said, "My mom told me to come up and pray over this building because God was sending someone to buy it!" We now own the building. I still get excited thinking about what the Lord did for us that day.

The following questions provide time for you to reflect on what God is saying to you. As you read through and answer the questions, open your mind and heart to the voice of God. I would even recommend praying and asking God to speak to you to answer these questions.

1. Think back on your life. Do you have any new realizations of how you have heard God in the past? Write down any experiences you can remember of hearing God's voice.

_____

_____

_____

_____

2. How have you experienced God or heard of God speaking through Scripture?

_____

_____

_____

3. How have you heard God or heard of God speaking through a still small voice?

_____

_____

_____

4. How have you heard God or heard of God speaking through worship?

_____

_____

_____

_____

_____

5. How have you heard God or heard of God speaking through vision?

_____

_____

_____

_____

_____

6. How have you heard God or heard of God speaking through Angels?

_____

_____

_____

_____

_____

7. How have you heard God or heard of God speaking through Orchestration?

_____

_____

_____

_____

_____

DAY 11

I knew God was calling me to begin my doctoral degree. I also knew we had a few bills to pay off before getting started. I wanted to start in November, but it looked like January would be the soonest I could start.

I remember it like it was yesterday. My husband and I were checking the mail at the post office, and I looked at him and said, "I wished I had an envelope from God with a letter and money in it that said, 'Here is the money for your first class. You may not use this to pay off bills or anything else. You must only use it to start your classes.'" He laughed and said, "That would be great."

About two weeks later, the deadline for starting in November was quickly approaching. I was beginning to doubt I heard God correctly. I was headed home from work. My phone rang, and it was my mom. She said, "Nikki, I have wanted to tell you something for a couple of months, but I felt God telling me the time wasn't right. However, today, God told me to call you. I want you to know that I have been putting back money, and I have enough for your first class. You can start in November. I don't want you to use this money for anything other than your class. You can't use it to pay bills, only your class." I had to immediately pull over because I was overwhelmed with tears of joy and thanksgiving. My husband and I had told no one of our conversation, and God spoke the exact words I had uttered to my husband through my mom and provided my mom with money to give me.

It is incredible to see how God orchestrates everyone's lives to help one another. It isn't just about the answers you get from hearing God. It is also how you impact the lives of others for God's kingdom. When we do not follow the call of God, it is not just us missing the blessing, but we are also robbing others of the blessing God wants to share with them through us. We are not the blessing, but when we allow the Holy Spirit to move and speak through us, God uses us as a tool to bless others.

Read Acts 9 to recall one of the greatest orchestrations.

The following questions provide time for you to reflect on what God is saying to you. As you read through and answer the questions, open your mind and heart to the voice of God. I would even recommend praying and asking God to speak to you to help answer these questions.

1. Describe your conversion.

_____

_____

_____

_____

2. What did it feel like to tell someone about your conversion? If you have never shared your experience, who could you share it with?

_____

_____

_____

_____

_____

3. How has God used you in the past? How did that make you feel?

_____

_____

_____

_____

4. Ask God to tell you how He can use you today or in the near future, and write it down?

_____

_____

_____

_____

5. What did you learn from God today?

_____

_____

_____

_____

_____

6. What can you thank God for today?

_____

_____

_____

_____

_____

7. Pray scripture over yourself to strengthen you as God sees fit to use you.

_____

_____

_____

_____

_____

DAY 12

In the summer of 1999 before we were married, my husband was driving home from work. A mutual friend had recently told him about a girl he should ask out. Fresh out of a relationship, he wasn't sure what to do, so he did the only thing he knew to do, and that was PRAY. While driving home and praying, asking God if he should ask this girl out or not, he came to a stop sign. He looked in his rearview mirror, and there I was in the car right behind him! He called me that night, and we scheduled our first date.

He had just started a new business, was building a house and was low on finances. So, he entered a fishing tournament in hopes of getting a little money to take me out. He won the tournament, and we had the money for the date. Five months later, we were married.

He set the example for our family. He was the first to listen to God's voice. With God's help, he has been and continues to be our leader, our protector, and our provider! I am forever thankful for his obedience and example.

Life is hard; making life decisions is even more challenging. I cannot encourage you enough to Trust God, His voice, and His call on your life. He will NEVER let you down. Sometimes, we may wonder how we know God is alive and real?

There are many ways, but one way I know is when I hear Truths from God's Word that I know God sent specifically for me. God knows my heart and my needs. He knows my fears and precisely how to speak to me so that I know He hears me and is going ahead of me in all situations. He knows your heart, your need, and your fears. He also knows precisely how to speak to you and let you know He hears you and is going ahead of you in all of your situations.

Read Mark 5:24-34. This is an example of true faith.
Three Truths I have learned over the years that help with faith:

1. Don't get in panic mode when God calls you to do something that scares you. Know instead that He is leading you.
2. Don't let fear cause you to cower down when God speaks to you; Trust Him.
3. Satan will try to make panic overcome your soul to keep you from doing what God calls you to.

The following questions provide time for you to reflect on what God is saying to you. As you read through and answer the questions, open your mind and heart to the voice of God. I would even recommend praying and asking God to speak to you to answer these questions.

1. What does panic mode look like to you when God calls you to do something that scares you?

_____

_____

_____

_____

2. How can you know God is leading you?

_____

_____

_____

_____

3. What would it look like to trust God instead of running from Him?

_____

_____

_____

_____

4. What does Satan do to put you in panic mode?

_____

_____

_____

_____

_____

5. What can you ask God to help you with today?

_____

_____

_____

_____

_____

6. What can you thank God for today?

_____

_____

_____

_____

_____

7. Pray scripture over yourself and your faith.

_____

_____

_____

_____

_____

DAY 13

Today is my favorite day. Today is the day we lay it all on the line for the Lord. We have experienced 12 days of getting to know our Savior. We have spent time communicating with Him over small things going on and big things in our lives. Most likely, you have felt weird and possibly uncomfortable, but hopefully, you have felt the presence of the Lord in your life.

Read Isaiah 37:14-20. Allow yourself to feel the power of laying it all out before the Lord.

Today is not about my life experiences or what I did to know the Lord more intimately. Today is about you and God. Take time to thank Him for all he has done in your life these past two weeks. I encourage you to write that down. Keep an answered prayer journal. When you are struggling, you can always go back and see all God has done for you.

_____

_____

_____

_____

_____

Now, take some time to write down things that you need God to give you direction on. This can be a list of things, it can be broad, but I encourage you to be as specific as you can. Take two weeks and pray about these things diligently. Lift them up to the Lord. Pray your scripture over yourself as you wait to see what the Lord says or where He Leads.

_____

_____

_____

_____

_____

_____

_____

_____

_____

_____

_____

DAY 14

Fasting can be a scary thought, especially on days two and three. Let me reassure you that fasting has been one of the most rewarding experiences in my Christian walk. I cannot explain the closeness it brings to my relationship with the Lord. Fasting brings a whole new meaning to reliance on God. Days two and three can make you consider whether or not fasting is the best life choice. I assure you; it is!

There are four main types of fasting: Fasting for repentance, fasting for direction, fasting for protection, and fasting out of gratitude. We will focus on fasting for direction with this 14-day devotion. I have received some of the most essential and miraculous revelations during fasting. So much that I must spend time in prayer to make sure fasting is appropriate. I often want to fast, but I never want to lose the reverence I feel when fasting. Many people regularly partake in spiritual fasting, which is perfectly fine if the Lord leads them to that. However, for me, regular spiritual fasting is not, at least at this point in my life, where I feel God is leading me. But, I am always open to God's direction on that.

Fasting for me is much more specific to divine intervention. With that being said, you need to spend time in prayer and relationship with God conversing about what He wants your fasting life to look like. Please do not base it on mine or anyone else's fasting. Make your fasting relationship yours and the Lords. Also, make sure you are in a healthy place before you fast. Feel free to check with your physician if you are concerned.

Read the following passages to see examples of fasting in the Bible: Deuteronomy 9:9-18 (fasting for direction), 2 Samuel 12:1-23 (fasting for repentance) he was forgiven but there were still consequences, 1 Kings 1:4-8 (fasting for protection), Esther 4:15-17 (fasting for safety), Daniel 6:18-23 (fasting for safety), Daniel 10:1-3 (fasting for answers to prayers), Matthew 4:1-2 (fasting to overcome temptation), Acts 13:2 (fasting out of gratitude).

It is essential to determine a fasting time before you start. I recommend a two-week fast, but you might want to start with a three, five, or seven-day fast. Then, work your way up to a 30-day fast, if God leads. It will be an amazing experience.

Below is a list of five different fasting options, four are spiritual fasts. This list is not in its entirety, but the ones I find best:

Entertainment Fasting: This fast includes eliminating tv, social media, book (except for the Bible), magazines, etc.

Intermittent Fasting: This fast is used for weight loss at times, but that should not be the purpose during a spiritual fast. This type of fasting requires eliminating food for a specific time frame, maybe sun up to sundown. There are many resources online.

Daniel Fasting: This fast eliminates all food except fruits, nuts, veggies, and water. There are many resources online.

Liquid Fasting: This fast eliminates any solid food. This fasting type is my fast of choice. I limit my consumption to water, coffee, juice, broth, liquid soups, and protein shakes (sometimes).

Complete Fasting: This fast eliminates all food. Water and juice are the only options allowed. I have completed this fast for 40 days. It was difficult, but it is what got me connected to the power and importance of fasting.

1. Take time to write down your initial thoughts about fasting. What scares you? What are you looking forward to?

_____

_____

_____

_____

_____

2. What time frame do you think you can commit to for your fasting? What type of fasting will you do?

_____

_____

_____

_____

3. How will you prepare?

_____

_____

_____

_____

4. What is your goal for fasting? What answer or direction do you need. And, how will you know if this answer or direction has been given to you from God?

_____

_____

_____

_____

CONCLUSION

It has been a pleasure to take this journey with you. I pray that your heart has been opened to hearing God's voice and His calls on your life. I hope you have been encouraged and empowered to take those next steps in trusting the Lord and growing in your relationship with Him. There will be difficult times that come but know the Lord is right beside you. He sees your future, and He knows your purpose. Cling to the one who sustains you. Be a Kingdom builder.

I wrote this book hoping that lives will be forever changed and that you will experience the same supernatural relationship with God that I have over the years. I would love to hear your stories of learning to hear God's voice, how God spoke to you, or where God has led you. May you and your family be blessed. And, remember what it says in Ephesians 3:20, "Our God is able to do exceedingly abundantly above all we ask or think."

Exceedingly Abundantly More!

WHAT'S NEXT...

We all have a call. I encourage you to use what you have learned these last 14 days and grow your relationship with God.

If you are ready to connect with God on a more substantial spiritual level, look for my upcoming book, 21 Days to Spiritual Convergence.

For more encouragement, follow me on:

Facebook: https://www.facebook.com/nikkiraderlifecoach

Instagram: @nrlifecoach

Website: nikkirader.com

ACKNOWLEDGEMENTS

I am deeply indebted to my parents for the solid foundation of Christ on which I stand and to my mom for her consistent encouragement, daily spiritual conversations, and proofreading.

I am grateful for my experiences with my daughter, her family, and my son, which have taught me so much.

Special thanks to my sister Rikki and my friends Amy, Dawn, Tammy, and Sarah for encouraging me over the years. Each of you has impacted me significantly.

I want to express my deepest gratitude to my friend Audria for allowing me to travel this life with her for over 25 years and for allowing me to use her supernatural experiences to share the greatness of the God we serve.

www.ingramcontent.com/pod-product-compliance
Lightning Source LLC
Chambersburg PA
CBHW071218120626
46546CB00006B/2617